EAST ANGLIA

·

In Verse and Prose

In the same series:

OXFORD and Oxfordshire In Verse edited by Antonia Fraser
CORNWALL In Verse edited by Peter Redgrove

General Editor: Emma Tennant

EAST ANGLIA

•

In Verse and Prose

•

Edited and with an introduction by

ANGUS WILSON

Research by Tony Garrett

Secker & Warburg · London

First published in England 1982 by
Martin Secker & Warburg Limited
54 Poland Street, London W1V 3DF

British Library Cataloguing in Publication Data

East Anglia in verse and prose
1. English literature 2. East Anglia
– Literary collections
I. Title II. Wilson, Angus *1913–*
820.8′03246 PR1111.E/

ISBN 0-436-57607-4

Photoset in Great Britain by
Rowland Phototypesetting Limited, Bury St Edmunds, Suffolk
and printed by St Edmundsbury Press,
Bury St Edmunds, Suffolk

This book is dedicated to
Albert and Ellen Revens
and
all those East Anglians
who have made us welcome.

CONTENTS

ACKNOWLEDGEMENTS

Frances Cornford: 'The Coast: Norfolk' from *Collected Poems* reprinted by permission of The Hutchinson Publishing Group Ltd.

Brendan Behan: Extract from *Borstal Boy* reprinted by permission of The Hutchinson Publishing Group Ltd.

Geoffrey Chaucer, translated by Theodore Morrison: 'The Reeve's Tale' from *The Portable Chaucer* reprinted by permission of Viking Penguin Inc.

The Rev. James Woodforde: extracts from *The Diary of a Country Parson*, published by Oxford University Press, reprinted by permission of the Beresford Estate.

John Betjeman: 'Norfolk' from *Collected Poems* reprinted by permission of Sir John Betjeman and John Murray (Publishers) Ltd.

George MacBeth: 'Yuletide in Norfolk' from *Poems from Oby* reprinted by permission of Secker & Warburg Ltd.

Elma Dean: 'Letter to Saint Peter', used with the article 'American Battlefield' in the *East Anglian Magazine* Vol. 9, No. 9, May 1950. Every effort has been made to trace Elma Dean.

Robert Lowell: 'Our Lady of Walsingham' from *Poems 1938–1949* reprinted by permission of Faber & Faber Ltd.

Andrew Motion: Part I of *Inland* reprinted by permission of Andrew Motion, The Cygnet Press and Carcanet Press.

Michael Riviere: 'On Lady Katherine Paston's Tomb at Oxnead' first published in *The Times Literary Supplement*, reprinted by permission of Michael Riviere.

R. N. Currey: 'King's Lynn' from *Writers of East Anglia* edited by Angus Wilson and published by Secker & Warburg Ltd., reprinted by permission of R. N. Currey.

Stephen Meadows: 'Beautiful Technical Language' from *Writers of East Anglia* edited by Angus Wilson and published by Secker & Warburg Ltd., reprinted by permission of Stephen Meadows.

ILLUSTRATION ACKNOWLEDGEMENTS

Harvesting in the fields near Cambridge and Remains of Walsingham Abbey are reproduced by permission of the Mansell Collection.

Ely Cathedral, Holkham Hall, King's Lynn and Yarmouth Old Pier are reproduced by permission of Mary Evans Picture Library.

INTRODUCTION

For the purposes of this anthology, I have taken East Anglia to mean Norfolk, Suffolk, and Cambridgeshire within its modern boundaries. The City of Cambridge, with its University, is not included here, as it would require a volume to itself.

I came to East Anglia fortuitously, seeking an immediate refuge in which to write. I have stayed nearly thirty years. Without my realising it, East Anglia has given to me a world of continuing enchantment – enchantment, subtle and in depth, which slowly and secretly becomes a part of one's very being. It is, I think, above all, a transfusion one receives of changing lights and shapes. We see it and know it at once in Constable and the other great landscape painters in this region. Only after I had lived here for some years did I realise that I could never in the future divorce forests, trees, commons, beaches, marshes, fens and all the exciting variety of wildlife and farm life associated with them from the sky and the clouds and, above all, the shadows and lights that they reflect in constant variety. Cathedrals, houses, streets, people inhabit this land of sky in unique relation; nowhere else approaches East Anglia for such strange, exciting change and interplay. We have no mountains here, no Alps no Lakeland hills and water to inspire the Romantic emotion; everything is more subtle, more visually intricate, a constant movement in and out of the natural scene and man's inner life, as may often be seen in the pieces of this anthology.

In this book we move from the wild North-Seascape to the busy and varied rural lives, both comic and tragic, of East Anglians; then comes the deep and religious heart of the land; with this is contrasted the outer world of great aristocratic households and the busy towns. But all this inevitably finds its roots in history – the Enclosures, Cromwell, Boudicca and the rest. We return full circle to celebration of the East Anglian scene and its meaning for the individual writer.

True, for long periods, Kingsley's wild North-easter drives all before it, but even here it is only a symbol of the great winds of invasion that have first devastated, then replenished East Anglia, so near to domestic England of the South and yet so far from it. Angles, Danes, Flemish weavers, Huguenots, have, in turn, menaced and yet proved fruitful. Have been repelled, then received and absorbed. To Brendan Behan, a prisoner here, the sea prospect seemed to have no limit but the rim of the world; to David Copperfield, on first sight, Yarmouth was the Pole; to Thomas Coke, looking out from his estate at Holkham, his nearest neighbour was the King of Denmark. Yet the sea-shore was for many centuries a wall, a gateway and, often, a silver lining to a prosperous hinterland. The herring or the bloater (silver-lined, of course) comes again and again to us as a symbol of the region. True the hinterland, too, changed dramatically in the seventeenth century, as forward-looking men, the Enclosers, brought doom to the eels of the fens – a drama that has inspired poetry from the anonymous 'Powte's Complaint' to the contemporary poetry of Andrew Motion. Yet without the Enclosures where would Marvell's Cromwell be? Each part of East Anglia has the same quality – at once remote, static and isolated, yet also changing over the years to open and communal.

It has bred great imaginative practical men, pioneers of agricultural advance – Coke of Norfolk, 'Turnip' Townshend, Arthur Young, Iveagh of Elveden, and, perhaps strangest of all, Rider Haggard. His absence from the anthology is no chance: his estates in Norfolk were the foundation of his enterprising work as an agricultural expert – into this went his considerable intellect; but his imagination, as he strode among his sheep and corn, was working in the faraway fields of African romance – of *She* and *Nada the Lily*.

The same two streams of inner and outer may surely be seen in the religious traditions of East Anglia, and in the many radical thinkers who have come from here. Walsingham shrine has inspired poets down to our great American contemporary, Robert Lowell. The seventeenth-century religious community at Little Gidding inspired T. S. Eliot, but alas, we were unable to include his poem for reasons of space. It is surely no chance that the sense of Norfolk's beautiful scene in his boyhood leads John Betjeman to reflect on the origin of his sense of evil. Yet Tom Paine had his birth in Thetford, and William Godwin found that all literate people knew his work when he came to Norfolk – 'I was nowhere a stranger.' But, then, the early stirrings of Magna Carta came from Bury Saint Edmunds, and Kett's rebellion began in Norfolk. Perhaps most remarkable in all this is the dominance of women: as mystics or religion's henchwomen – Etheldrida, Julian of Norwich, Marjorie Kempe; as radical pioneers – Anna Letitia Barbauld, a teacher at Palgrave, and Harriet Martineau, surely the first emancipated woman to mock and deride Women's Lib. Descendants, of course, of Queen Boudicca, great leader, great victim, inspirer of poems.

There is a lonely darkness among the people of this region, which has given birth to many poems – Eugene Aram, above all, and Peter Grimes; and, without crime, Clare's deep sense of loss. But there is also a communal blackness – the presence of rogues: none so fine in treatment as Chaucer's in 'The Reeve's Tale', where the lonely Gothic mood of Aram the murderer or Grimes has no place, and violent crime gives way to skilful bedroom farce. For, finally, community has its gaiety and zest in this area also, whether in gleaning or in the natural instinctive play, as when the Suffolk girl joins Kemp in his fantastic dance from London to Norwich.

Sometimes one wonders whether the idea of idyllic, virtuous country retreat is not just Londoners' escapism. Certainly it was at the ebb of the economic fortunes of the beautiful Waveney valley countryside in late Victorian times that Trollope chose to end his wonderful novel of London's corruption with the forward-looking last chapter, called 'Down in Suffolk', and to the same remote region that Henry James took his young heroine, Nanda, in *The Awkward Age* to escape the snares of the 'nineties London smart set. Yet Rupert Brooke's real sense of perfection in 'Grantchester' is surely no simple escapism: here is pastoral inspiration, peace, where East Anglian skies offer shelter not threat.

ANGUS WILSON

Ode to the North-East Wind

WELCOME, wild North-easter!
Shame it is to see
Odes to every zephyr;
Ne'er verse to thee.
Welcome, black North-easter!
O'er the German foam;
O'er the Danish moorlands.
From thy frozen home.
Tired we are of summer,
Tired of gaudy glare,
Showers soft and steaming,
Hot and breathless air.
Tired of listless dreaming,
Through the lazy day:
Jovial wind of winter
Turns us out to play!
Sweep the golden reed-beds;
Crisp the lazy dyke;
Hunger into madness
Every plunging pike.
Fill the lake with wild-fowl;
Fill the marsh with snipe;
While on dreary moorlands
Lonely curlew pipe.
Through the black fir-forest
Thunder harsh and dry,
Shattering down the snow-flakes
Off the curdled sky.
Hark! The brave North-easter!
Breast-high lies the scent,
On by holt and headland,
Over heath and bent.
Chime, ye dappled darlings,
Through the sleet and snow.
Who can over-ride you?

* * *

While our skates are ringing
  O'er the frozen streams.
Let the luscious South-wind
  Breathe in lovers' sighs,
While the lazy gallants
  Bask in ladies' eyes.
What does he but soften
  Heart alike and pen?
Tis the hard grey weather
  Breeds hard English men.
What's the soft South-wester?
  'Tis the ladies' breeze,
Bringing home their true-loves
  Out of all the seas:
But the black North-easter,
  Through the snowstorm hurled,
Drives our English hearts of oak
  Seaward round the world.
Come, as came our fathers,
  Heralded by thee,
Conquering from the eastward.
  Lords by land and sea.
Come; and strong within us
  Stir the Vikings' blood;
Bracing brain and sinew;
  Blow, thou wind of God!

CHARLES KINGSLEY (1819–1875)

The Coast: Norfolk

As on the highway's quiet edge
He mows the grass beside the hedge,
The old man has for company
The distant, grey, salt-smelling sea,
A poppied field, a cow and calf,
The finches on the telegraph.

Across his faded back a hone,
He slowly, slowly scythes alone
In silence of the wind-soft air,
With ladies' bedstraw everywhere,
With whitened corn, and tarry poles,
And far-off gulls like risen souls.

FRANCES CORNFORD (1886–1960)

From *Peter Grimes*

. . . Rough was the passage and the time was long;
His liquor fail'd, and Peter's wrath arose,—
No more is known—the rest we must suppose,
Or learn of Peter: Peter says he 'spied
The stripling's danger, and for harbour tried:
Meantime the fish, and then th'apprentice died.'
The pitying women raised a clamour round,
And weeping said, 'Thou hast thy 'prentice drown'd.'
Now the stern man was summon'd to the Hall,
To tell his tale before the burghers all:
He gave th' account; profess'd the lad he loved,
And kept his brazen features all unmoved.
The mayor himself with tone severe replied,
'Henceforth with thee shall never boy abide;
Hire thee a freeman, whom thou durst not beat,
But who, in thy despite, will sleep and eat:
Free thou art now!—again shouldst thou appear,
Thou'lt find thy sentence, like thy soul, severe.'
Alas! for Peter not a helping hand,
So was he hated, could he now command;
Alone he row'd his boat, alone he cast
His nets beside, or made his anchor fast:
To hold a rope, or hear a curse was none;
He toil'd and rail'd: he groan'd and swore alone.
Thus by himself compell'd to live each day,
To wait for certain hours the tide's delay;
At the same times the same dull views to see,
The bounding marsh-bank and the blighted tree;
The water only, when the tides were high,
When low, the mud half cover'd and half dry;
The sunburnt tar that blisters on the planks,
And bank-side stakes in their uneven ranks;
Heaps of entangled weeds that slowly float,
As the tide rolls by the impeded boat.
When tides were neap, and, in the sultry day,

Through the tall bounding mud-banks made their way,
Which on each side rose swelling, and below
The dark warm flood ran silently and slow;
There anchoring, Peter chose from man to hide,
There hang his head, and view the lazy tide
In its hot slimy channel slowly glide;
Where the small eels that left the deeper way
For the warm shore, within the shallows play;
Where gaping mussels, left upon the mud,
Slope their slow passage to the fallen flood;—
Here dull and hopeless he'd lie down and trace
How sidelong crabs had scrawl'd their crooked race,
Or sadly listen to the tuneless cry
Of fishing gull or clanging golden-eye;
What time the sea-birds to the marsh would come,
And the loud bittern from the bulrush home,
Gave from the salt ditch side the bellowing boom:
He nursed the feelings these dull scenes produce,
And loved to stop beside the opening sluice;
Where the small stream, confined in narrow bound,
Ran with a dull, unvaried, sadd'ning sound;
Where all, presented to the eye or ear,
Oppress'd the soul with misery, grief, and fear.
   Besides these objects, there were places three,
Which Peter seem'd with certain dread to see;
When he drew near them, he would turn from each,
And loudly whistle till he pass'd the reach.
   A change of scene to him brought no relief,
In town, 'twas plain, men took him for a thief:
The sailors' wives would stop him in the street,
And say, 'Now, Peter, thou'st no boy to beat;'
Infants at play, when they perceived him, ran,
Warning each other,—'That's the wicked man!'
   He growl'd an oath, and in an angry tone
Cursed the whole place, and wish'd to be alone.

*   *   *

Cold nervous tremblings shook his sturdy frame,
And strange disease—he couldn't say the name;
Wild were his dreams, and oft he rose in fright,
Waked by his view of horrors in the night—
Horrors that would the sternest minds amaze,
Horrors that demons might be proud to raise:
And though he felt forsaken, grieved at heart,
To think he lived from all mankind apart;
Yet, if a man approach'd, in terror he would start.

GEORGE CRABBE (1754–1832)

Peter Grimes *inspired Benjamin Britten's opera of the same name.*

I rolled over beside Charlie. 'Jesus, I'd love a swim,' said I.

'I should like one myself, Paddy, not 'alf, I wouldn't.'

'I wouldn't mind a swim, either,' said Jock. 'It's a pity about the beach being out of bounds.'

'Yerra, who the fughing hell would know a ha'p'orth about it, if we just snaked down the five of us?' said I impatiently.

'Ah'm game,' said a soft voice beside me. It was 538 Jones, a young kid of sixteen from Stoke-on-Trent. He had a head of disorderly fair hair, and sleepy blue eyes, and I liked him because he was the next number to me.

'Who bloody asked you whether you were game or not?' said Charlie.

'You don't own the bloody North Sea, does you?' asked 538 Jones, setting his face.

'Now, for Jasus' sake,' said I, 'nark the arguments. There's plenty of water down there for everyone and the only thing is, how to get down to it, without being tumbled by the screws, and number two, how to get a swim, without being blown to shit by these mines when we do get down there.'

'I been down there drawing sand for the farm party and I know a place where there's no mines. We drove 'orse and cart over it, so there can't be.'

* * *

'Good man yourself,' said I. 'Let's snake off down there and off we go. There's no more to it. Jones, lead the way.'

He brought us down through an orchard, and the leaves were heavy and glinted in the sun, as if they had a coat of synthetic green enamel on them.

It was dark under the trees till we came out on a sand hill.

'By God, I can smell the sea,' said I.

'We're nearly there,' said 538 Jones.

I sang a bit of a song:

'The sea, oh, the sea, a ghradh gheal mo chroi,
Oh, long may it roll between England and me,
God help the poor Scotchmen, they'll never be free,
But we're entirely surrounded by water.'

Charlie put his hand on my shoulder and smiled. 'You're a rum bastard, Paddy.'

'Them,' said I, 'are the truest words you ever said.'

We walked over some more sand heaps and, at last, 538 Jones stood on the top, looking down at the sea, as if he'd made it himself.

We stood beside him and looked down at the sun on the water.

'Me life on you, Jonesy,' said I. 'You're like "Stout Cortez when with eagle eyes, he stared at the Pacific—and all his men looked at each other with a wild surmise, silent, upon a peak in Darien." By Jasus, this equals any fughing Darien.'

There was no beach, like Killiney, but a stony stretch of pebbles that would remind you of the people of the place, but the water, glittering and dancing, stretched away out in front of us, with no limit but the rim of the world and it was green and blue farther out; there was a bit of a concrete breakwater, that I picked for a dive.

I caught 538 Jones by the arm, and said, 'Long life to you, 538 Jones, and a bed in heaven to you, but you're a great young fellow.'

'Who's going to break the ice?' said Jock.

'Maybe Joe would go in first,' said I.

'I only came down 'ere for the pleasure of seeing you sods drown,' said Joe. 'The only time I ever 'ad a bath was with a young judy from Birmingham way. She was only a week in London. I broke 'er in.'

'I'm afraid we can't provide that sort of accommodation for you here,' said I.

'You're a filthy sod and no mistake,' said Charlie to Joe.

'You could 'ardly call me a filthy sod for 'aving a bath.'

'Whatever kind of a sod you are,' said Jock, 'we can't stand 'ere all day arguing the toss.' He took off his jacket.

'There's a little stretch of beach here,' said 538 Jones, 'from where we cart sand.'

We moved down to the sand and a nice little beach it was; we took off our clothes, except Chewlips, who said he was only having a paddle.

The sun beat down on us, naked, and we stretched our arms under our heads.

'You right there, Paddy?' asked Charlie.

'I'm going in off that bit of concrete. You and Jock and Jonesy go in first and see what depth it is. Joe can't swim, so he can follow the rest of yous.'

'I'm away,' said Jock, blessing himself and running straight for the water, till he stumbled into his depth and started swimming. He dived and came up treading water, and shouted, 'It's smashing!'

'Come on, kid,' said Charlie to 538 Jones, and the two of them ran down together and into the water.

I stood on the concrete and shouted to Joe, 'Now, there's your depth.'

Joe blessed himself and waded in, and stood when the water reached his thighs. 'I never know what to do when I'm this far. I'm like an 'ore at a christening.'

'Go on in out of that,' I shouted. 'I'll be in, in a second.'

He went out to where the others were, but slowly. 538 Jones was delighted with himself, coming up and diving straight down with his bare arse turning over on the surface, till he came up and Charlie and he were doing a sort of dance, treading water and laughing and shouting.

'You're O.K., Paddy, you've got plenty of depth there for a dive.'

I looked out over the sea, and up at the sun and the sky, and over to where they were swimming, their shoulders over the water, as they waited for me to dive, blessed myself and balanced on the balls of my feet.

'*Introibo ad altare Dei*,' shouted Joe.

'*Ad Deum Qui laetificat juventutem meam*,' I shouted, and dived.

I swam under water till I came up in the middle of them. I dived under Charlie, caught him and nearly threw him out of the water.

'Let go, you Irish bastard,' he shouted, spitting sea water into my face. I swam away and lay back in the sea, looking up at the sun and laughing.

538 Jones and Charlie and I dived and swam under water towards Joe,

looking towards each other, as if this was where we'd always lived, a world of naked, waving limbs and silent, open eyes.

BRENDAN BEHAN (1923–1964)

From Borstal Boy *(1958). Behan spent time in Hollesley Bay Borstal, Suffolk.*

There was an old person of Cromer
Who stood on one leg to read Homer;
When he found he grew stiff, he jumped over the cliff
Which concluded that Person of Cromer.

EDWARD LEAR (1812–1888)

The Dream of Eugene Aram

'Twas in the prime of summer time,
An evening calm and cool,
And four-and-twenty happy boys
Came bounding out of school:
There were some that ran, and some that leapt,
Like troutlets in a pool.

Away they sped with gamesome minds,
And souls untouched by sin;
To a level mead they came, and there
They drave the wickets in:
Pleasantly shone the setting sun
Over the town of Lynn.

Like sportive deer they coursed about,
And shouted as they ran,—
Turning to mirth all things of earth,
As only boyhood can;
But the Usher sat remote from all,
A melancholy man!

His hat was off, his vest apart,
To catch heaven's blessed breeze;
For a burning thought was in his brow,
And his bosom ill at ease:
So he leaned his head on his hands, and read
The book between his knees!

Leaf after leaf he turned it o'er,
Nor ever glanced aside,
For the peace of his soul he read that book
In the golden eventide:
Much study had made him very lean,
And pale, and leaden-eyed.

At last he shut the ponderous tome,
With a fast and fervent grasp
He strained the dusky covers close,
And fixed the brazen hasp:
'O, God! could I close my mind,
And clasp it with a clasp!'

Then leaping on his feet upright,
Some moody turns he took,—
Now up the mead, then down the mead,
And past a shady nook,—
And, lo! he saw a little boy
That pored upon a book!

'My gentle lad, what is't you read—
Romance or fairy fable?
Or is it some historic page,
Of kings and crowns unstable?'
The young boy gave an upward glance,—
'It is "The Death of Abel." '

The Usher took six hasty strides,
As smit with sudden pain,—
Six hasty strides beyond the place,
Then slowly back again;
And down he sat beside the lad,
And talked with him of Cain;

And, long since then, of bloody men,
Whose deeds tradition saves;
Of lonely folk cut off unseen,
And hid in sudden graves;
Of horrid stabs in groves forlorn,
And murders done in caves;

And how the sprites of injured men
  Shriek upward from the sod,—
Ay, how the ghostly hand will point
  To show the burial clod;
And unknown facts of guilty acts
  Are seen in dreams from God!

He told how murderers walk the earth
  Beneath the curse of Cain,—
With Crimson clouds before their eyes,
  And flames about their brain
For blood has left upon their souls
  Its everlasting stain!

'And well,' quoth he, 'I know, for truth,
  Their pangs must be extreme,—
Woe, woe, unutterable woe,—
  Who spill life's sacred stream!
For why? Methought, last night, I wrought
  A murder, in a dream!

'One that had never done me wrong—
  A feeble man and old;
I led him to a lonely field,—
  The moon shone clear and cold:
Now here, said I, this man shall die
  And I will have his gold!

'Two sudden blows with a ragged stick,
  And one with a heavy stone,
One hurried gash with a hasty knife,—
  And then the deed was done:
There was nothing lying at my foot
  But lifeless flesh and bone!

'Nothing but lifeless flesh and bone,
That could not do me ill;
And yet I feared him all the more,
For lying there so still:
There was a manhood in his look,
That murder could not kill!

* * *

'And now, from forth the frowning sky,
From the heaven's topmost height,
I heard a voice—the awful voice
Of the blood-avenging sprite:—
"Thou guilty man! take up thy dead
And hide it from my sight!"

'I took the dreary body up,
And cast it in a stream—
A sluggish water, black as ink,
The depth was so extreme:—
My gentle Boy, remember this
Is nothing but a dream!

'Down went the corse with a hollow plunge,
And vanished in the pool;
Anon I cleansed my bloody hands,
And washed my forehead cool,
And sat among the urchins young,
That evening, in the school.

* * *

'Oh, God! that horrid, horrid dream
Besets me now awake!
Again—again, with dizzy brain,
The human life I take;
And my red right hand grows raging hot,
Like Cranmer's at the stake.

'And still no peace for the restless clay
Will wave or mould allow;
The horrid thing pursues my soul,—
It stands before me now!'
The fearful Boy looked up, and saw
Huge drops upon his brow.

That very night, while gentle sleep
The urchin eyelids kissed,
Two stern-faced men set out from Lynn,
Through the cold and heavy mist:
And Eugene Aram walked between,
With gyves upon his wrist.

THOMAS HOOD (1799–1845)

Aram was arrested in 1758 for murder whilst a master at the Grammar School, King's Lynn, Norfolk

The Reeve's Tale

At Trumpington, near Cambridge, a brook flows;
Across this brook, moreover, a bridge goes,
And on the said brook stands a mill as well,
And sober truth is all this that I tell,
A miller lived there once for many a day
Who dressed up like a peacock. He could play
The bagpipes, wrestle, shoot his bow, and fish,
Mend nets, and lathe a wooden cup or dish.
He wore a long knife always at his belt;
Keen as a sharpened sword its edges felt.
A fancy dagger too he kept upon him,
And no man dared to put a finger on him.
He kept a Sheffield blade inside his hose.
He had a round face and a flattened nose.
His skull had no more hair than a bald ape.
He went to market looking for a scrape,
And anyone who was bold enough to lay
A hand on him he swore he'd soon repay,
He was for fact a thief of corn and meal,
And sly at that, well versed in how to steal.
He was christened Simon; Simkin by nickname.
As for his wife, from noble kin she came.
Her father was the parson of the town,
And handsome was the dowry he paid down,
For Simkin with his blood would be allied.
She was brought up in a convent; in his pride
Simkin refused to take a wife, he said,
Unless she were a maiden and well bred,
To keep up his position as a yeoman.
Proud as a jay she was and pert, this woman.
They made a sight together, did this pair.
On saints' day he would march in front of her,
The muffler of his hood tied round his head
While she came after in a cape of red,
And Simkin sported long hose of the same.

No one dares speak to her except as 'Dame,'
And non so hardy walking by the way
Who dared make love or even so much as play,
Unless he would be killed, with Simkin's wife,
For fear of Simkin's cutlass or his knife.
These jealous men are dangerous, as we know;
At least they want their wives to think them so.
She suffered a smirch by being a priest's daughter,
And so she was as snotty as ditch water,
Hoity-toity and down-her-nose to spare.
A lady ought to carry her self with care,
She thought, what for the duty of maintaining
Her kinship and her stock of convent training.
Between them they produced a daughter, grown
To twenty or so, and save for her alone
No other children except one, a mere
Babe in the cradle, of some half a year.
She was a plump, well-rounded wench, this lass,
Her nose was flat, her blue eyes clear as glass,
Her buttocks broad, her breasts were round and high.
But she had lovely hair, and that's no lie.
This parson, seeing that the girl was fair,
Had it in mind to name her as his heir,
Both of his goods and dwelling in addition.
He made her marriage hard, for his ambition
Was to bestow her, hand and property,
On blood that came of worthy ancestry.
The things that are Holy Church's must be spent
On blood that Holy Church owns by descent;
He would not leave his holy blood in the lurch
Although he might devour the Holy Church.
A heavy toll this miller took, past doubt,
Of wheat and barley all the land about.
He cheated the great college worst of all
That stands in Cambridge, King's or Soler Hall,

For he was given their malt and wheat to grind.
　They happened, on a certain day, to find
Their steward sick, and in a stupor lying.
They thought for certain that he must be dying,
And so this miller stole both meal and corn
More than he ever had since he was born
A hundredfold; he thieved it courteously
Before, but now he stole outrageously.
The provost stormed and raised a great affair,
But all this gave the miller little care.
He talked big, swearing, 'Not so,' on his oath.
　Two poor young students at that time were both
Residing in this hall of which I speak.
They loved their fun, and they were full of cheek,
And merely for a jaunt they busily
Begged the provost to let them go and see
Their corn ground at the mill. Each bet his neck
The miller wouldn't cost them half a peck
Whether by force or sleight he tried to thieve.
At last the provost granted them his leave.
　John was the name of one, Alan the other.
Their birthplace was the same, a town called Strother,
Far to the north, I cannot tell you where.
　Alan gathered his stuff for this affair,
And got a horse to put the grain sack on.
So off went Alan the student, off went John.
Each with a sword and buckler by his side.
John knew the way, he did not need a guide,
And at the mill the grain sack down he set.
Alan spoke first. 'Simkin,' he said, 'well met!
How are your lovely daughter and your wife?'
　'Alan!' said Simkin. 'Welcome, on my life,
And also John. What are you doing here?'
　'Simkin,' said John, 'without a slave, no fear,
A man slaves for himself, or he's a fool.

Necessity, say the learned, knows no rule.
Our steward, I expect, will soon be dead
His molars ache so steadily in his head.
That's why I'm here, and Alan too. We've come
To grind our corn, and then to carry it home.
Help us get off as quickly as may be.'
'Just as you want it,' Simkin said. 'Trust me.
What will you do while this is going on?'
'By God, right by the hopper,' answered John,
'I'll stand, and see just how the corn goes in.
I've never watched yet, by my father's kin,
The way the hopper jiggles to and fro.'
'Is that,' said Alan, 'what you're going to do?
I'll be down underneath then, by my hide,
And notice how the grain comes down the slide
Into the trough. That's what I'll do for sport,
For, John, the fact is that I'm of your sort,
I am as bad a miller as you can be.'
The miller smiled at their simplicity,
And thought, 'So that's it, that's their stratagem!
They fancy no one can hornswoggle them.
But yet I'll let them have some dust in the eye
For all the sleight in their philosophy.
The better the trap, no matter how sly they make it.
The more I'll pilfer when I'm ready to take it.
Instead of flour I'll give them only bran.
"The greatest scholar is not the wisest man,"
As one time to the wolf remarked the mare.
For all their cunning a fig is what I care.'
Out through the doorway he slipped quietly
When he perceived his time, in secrecy,
And up and down he looked until he found
The students' horse, where it was standing bound
Behind the mill beneath a clump of trees.
Up to the horse as easy as you please

He went, and stripped the bridle off, and when
The horse was loose he started for the fen
Where there were wild mares running, and thundered in,
'Wehee,' whinnying on through thick and thin.
  This miller came back, not a word he spoke,
But with the students he began to joke
And worked until the corn was all well ground,
And when the meal was in the sack and bound
This John goes out and finds no horse at all.
'Help! Help!' and 'God's bones!' he began to call.
'Our horse is gone! Come out here, Alan, man!
Step on your feet! Get going, if you can!
Our provost's palfrey lost—here's a fine deal!'
  This Alan, he forgot both corn and meal,
His husbandry was wholly put to rout.
'What, where was he heading?' he began to shout.
  The miller's wife came leaping in on the run.
'Off to the fen,' she said, 'your horse has gone
With the wild mares, as fast as he can go,
And no thanks to the hand that tied him so.
He should have put a better knot in the reins.'
  'Alas,' this John said, 'Alan, for Christ's pains,
Put down your sword, and I'll put mine down too.
A roe can't run, by God, the way I do.
He can't shake both of us, he won't be able.
God's heart, why didn't you put him in the stable?
God, Alan, you're a fool! Look what you've done!'
  Hell bent away these hapless scholars run
Straight toward the fen, Alan, and with him John.
The miller, when he saw that they were gone,
Took of their flour half a bushel or so
And told his wife to knead it into dough.
'I think these students had their fears,' he said,
'But a miller can beat a scholar, head for head,
For all his knowledge. Let them go their way!

Look, where they go! Yes, let the children play.
They'll work before they catch him, I'll be bound!'
   These luckless students ran and thrashed around
With 'Whoa! Whoa! Stand! This way! Behind, keep clear!
You go and whistle, and I'll hold him here!'
To cut it short, until the very night
They could not, though they worked with all their might,
Lay hands upon their nag, he ran so fast,
Until they caught him in a ditch at last.
   Weary and wet as a cow is in the rain
Alan, and with him John, came back again.
'A curse,' said John, 'on the day that I was born!
Now we'll be in for ribbing and for scorn.
Our meal is stolen, men will call us "fool,"
Yes, both the provost and our friends at school,
And specially the miller, damn the day.'
   With Bayard the horse in hand along the way
Back to the mill, thus John moaned in his ire.
He found the miller sitting by his fire,
For it was night. No farther could they go,
But begged him for the love of God to show
Some comfort and some shelter for their penny.
   The miller answered them, 'If there is any,
Such as it is, you two shall have your part.
My house is small, but with your scholar's art
You can by syllogisms make a place
A mile wide out of twenty feet of space.
See if there's room in this place for us each,
Or as your way is, puff it up with speech.'
   'Now, by St. Cuthbert, always a bright word,
Simon,' said John. 'Well answered! I have heard "A man must
always take one of two things,
Such as he finds, or else such as he brings."
But specially, and this I beg you most,
Get us some meat and drink, make cheer, good host,

And we will pay in full, you understand.
A man can't lure a hawk with empty hand.
Look, here's our silver, ready to be spent.'
His daughter off to town the miller sent
For ale and bread, and roasted them a goose,
And tied their horse, no more to wander loose.
In his own room he made them up a bed
With sheets and Chalon blankets neatly spread
Not more than ten or twelve feet from his own.
His daughter in the same room slept alone,
All by herself, in another bed close by.
It was the best that could be done—and why?
There were no roomier quarters, that was clear.
They talked and ate their supper with good cheer,
And pulled hard on the strong ale, as seemed best.
And when the midnight came, they went to rest.
This miller was well oiled by now. His head,
He had drunk so much, was pale instead of red.
He hiccups, and his voice comes through his nose
As if he had a cold. To bed he goes,
And with him goes his wife, jolly and gay,
Light in the head and frisking like a jay
So well her merry whistle had been wet.
Under the footboard of their bed they set
The cradle, where the child could nurse and rock.
And when they finish all that's in the crock
The daughter goes to bed; when she is gone
To bed goes Alan and to bed goes John.
And that was all—they did not need a drug.
This sleeping miller had so plied the jug
He snorted like a horse, nor did he mind
What might be happening to his tail behind.
His wife kept up a counterbass in style.
You could have heard them snore for half a mile.
The wench snored with them, too, for company.

Alan, who listened to this melody,
Poked John and said, 'Are you sleeping through this row?
Have you ever heard such music before now?
Here's a fine service to wind up the day
Between them all! I hope they burn away
With itch. Did ever such a racket rend
A poor man's ears? The best of a bad end
I'll give them, though. I see I'll have no rest
All the long night; no matter, it's for the best.
For, John, by all the wealth of church or bench,
If I can work it, I'm going to lay that wench.
The law itself some easement offers us,
For John, there is a maxim that goes thus:
If in one point of law a man's aggrieved,
Then in some other he shall be relieved.
Our corn is stolen; that we can't gainsay,
And we've been in a bad fix this whole day.
Now since my loss is past all cancellation,
I will accept instead some compensation.
By the soul of God,' he said, 'it shall be so.'
'Alan,' this John replied, 'think twice! You know
This miller is a dangerous man,' he said.
'And if he wakes and jumps up out of bed
He may do both of us an injury.'
'I hold him,' Alan answered, 'a mere flea.'
He rose, and toward the wench began to creep.
This wench lay stretched out flat and fast asleep.
He got so near she could not bat an eye
Before it was too late to raise a cry.
To cut the story short, they were at one.
Now make hay, Alan, and we'll turn to John.
This John lay quiet for a moment or so.
He brooded to himself, and nursed his woe.
'This is a wicked prank, and no escape.
I see that I'm no better than an ape.

My pal, here, for his troubles and his harms
Has got the miller's daughter in his arms.
He took a chance, and now his needs are fed
While like a sack of chaff I lie in bed.
People will joke about this exploit soon,
And I'll pass for a fool and a poltroon.
I'll rise and take my chance too, come what may.
For "nothing venture, nothing have," they say.'
He rose, and to the cradle cautiously
He went, and picked it up, and quietly
He put it by his bed's foot on the floor.
Soon after this the good wife ceased to snore.
She went out for a leak, and coming back,
She missed the cradle. She felt first on one tack,
Then on another, but cradle there was none.
'Mercy,' she said, 'I've almost been undone!
I almost got into the students' bed.
Eh, bless me, then I would have been ill sped!'
And on she gropes until her fingers find
The cradle and the bed, and in her mind
She had no thought of anything but good,
For there right by the bed the cradle stood,
And since the night was dark, she could not see,
But by the student crawled in trustfully,
And lay quite still, and would have gone to sleep.
Presently John the student, with a leap,
Pitched into this good woman. Year in, year out,
She had not had for long so merry a bout,
For hard and deep he went; he thrust like mad.
Such was the jolly life these students had
Until the cocks were tuning up their choir
For the third time. Alan began to tire
As dawn came near, for he had worked all night.
'Molly,' he whispered, 'it will soon be light.
I can't stay any longer at your side.

But sweetheart, always, though I walk or ride,
I am your own forever, till I die.'
'Now, darling, go,' said Molly, 'and good-by.
But wait, I'm going to tell you something still.
On the way home, as you go past the mill,
Stop at the door, and there, right in behind,
A good half-bushel loaf of bread you'll find.
Kneaded it was and baked from your own meal,
The very same I helped my father steal.
And now God keep you safe, sweetheart, God keep—'
And she was almost in a state of weep.
Alan got up. 'Before it's day, I ought
To crawl in with my crony here,' he thought,
And promptly felt the cradle with his hand.
'I'm all turned round, I don't know where I stand.
My head is fuzzy with my work tonight.
By God, I haven't got my bearings right.
The cradle makes it certain I've gone wrong.
Here's where the miller and his wife belong.'
And as the devil would have it, groped his way
Straight to the bed in which the miller lay.
And in with John, or so he thought, he eased him,
And lay down by the miller instead, and seized him
Around the neck, and speaking softly said:
'Wake up, you John, wake up, you dull swine's head!
Listen, for Christ's soul, to some noble sport,
For, by St. James, although it has been short,
Flat on her back, three times in this one night,
I've rolled the miller's daughter, while for fright,
You lay here!'
'Have you so,' the miller said,
'False thief? God's dignity, you shall be dead!
Traitor! You dared abuse a daughter of mine,
False scholar, and she comes of such a line?'
And he seized Alan by the Adam's-apple,

And Alan desperately began to grapple
With him, and let him have it on the nose,
And down the miller's chest a red stream flows
And on the floor, with nose smashed and teeth broke
They heave and roll like two pigs in a poke,
And up they get and down again they go
Till on a stone the miller stubbed his toe
And took a backward tumble on his wife,
Who had no notion of this frenzied strife,
For she had quickly dozed off with this John
Who had not slept all night for what went on;
But with the fall her eyes popped open wide,
And 'Holy cross of Bromholm, help!' she cried.
'Into thy hands, O Lord—on thee I call!
Wake, Simon! Fiends and devils on me fall!
My ribs are burst. Help! I'm as good as dead.
Someone is on my belly and my head.
Help, Simkin, for the wicked students fight!'
  This John sprang up as quickly as he might
And here and there along the walls he fumbled
To find a staff; and out she also tumbled
And knew the right nooks better than he could,
And by the wall she found a stick of wood,
And saw a tiny glimmering of light
Where through a crack the moon was shining bright,
And by this glint of light she saw the two,
But could not tell for certain who was who
Except for something pale that she made out.
Seeing this thing of white, she had no doubt
It was a nightcap that the student wore.
Closer and closer with her stick she bore,
Thinking to hit this Alan a good bop,
And fetched the miller one on his bald top.
He went down with a yelp, 'Ow, I am dying!'
These students beat him up and left him lying,

And quickly dressed and got their meal and horse
And set out promptly on their homeward course,
And at the mill they found, as Molly had said,
Well-baked, their good half-bushel loaf of bread.
So this proud miller got himself a beating,
And lost his labor, what with all his cheating,
And paid for every bit they had to sup,
Alan and John, who soundly beat him up.
His wife got hers, so did his daughter too.
This comes of the cheating that false millers do!
True are the words of this old proverb still:
'Let him not look for good whose works are ill,'
For tricked himself shall every trickster be.
And now may God, throned high in majesty,
Bring us, both great and small, into His glory!
Thus I have paid the Miller with my story.

GEOFFREY CHAUCER (c. 1340–1400)

From The Canterbury Tales, *translated by Theodore Morrison.*

Forth comes the Maid, and like the morning smiles;
The Mistress too, and follow'd close by *Giles*.
A friendly tripod forms their humble seat,
With pails bright scour'd, and delicately sweet.
Where shadowing elms obstruct the morning ray,
Begins the work, begins the simple lay;
The full-charg'd udder yields its willing streams,
While *Mary* sings some lover's amorous dreams;
And crouching *Giles* beneath a neighbouring tree
Tugs o'er his pail and chants with equal glee;
Whose hat with tatter'd brim, of nap so bare,
From the cow's side purloins a coat of hair,
A mottled ensign of his harmless trade,
An unambitious, peaceable cockade.
As unambitious too that cheerful aid
The Mistress yields beside her rosy Maid;
With joys she views her plenteous reeking store,
And bears a brimmer to the dairy door;
Her Cows dismiss'd, the luscious mead to roam,
Till eve again recal them loaded home.
And now the DAIRY claims her choisest care,
And half her household find employment there:
Slow rolls the churn, its load of clogging cream
At once foregoes its quality and name:
From knotty particles first floating wide
Congealing butter's dash'd from side to side;
Streams of new milk through flowing coolers stray,
And snow-white curd abounds, and wholesome whey.
Due north th' unglazed windows, cold and clear,
For warming sunbeams are unwelcome here.
Brisk goes the work beneath each busy hand,
And *Giles* must trudge, whoever gives command;
A *Gibeonite*, that serves them all by turns:
He drains the pump, from him the faggot burns;
From him the noisy Hogs demand their food;

While at his heels run many a chirping brood,
Or down his path in expectation stand,
With equal claims upon his strewing hand.
Thus wastes the morn, till each with pleasure sees
The bustle o'er, and press'd the new-made cheese.
   Unrivall'd stands thy country CHEESE, O *Giles!*
Whose very name alone engenders smiles;
Whose fame abroad by every tongue is spoke,
The well-known butt of many a flinty joke,
That pass like current coin the nation through;
And, ah! experience proves the satire true.
Provision's grave, thou ever-craving mart.
Dependant, huge Metropolis! where Art
Her poring thousands stows in breathless rooms.
Midst pois'nous smokes and steams, and rattling looms;
Where Grandeur revels in unbounded stores;
Restraint, a slighted stranger at their doors!
Thou, like a whirlpool, drain'st the countries round,
Till London market, London price, resound
Through every town, round every passing load,
And dairy produce throngs the eastern road:
Delicious veal, and butter, every hour,
From Essex lowlands, and the banks of Stour;
And further far, where numerous herds repose,
From Orwell's brink, from Waveney, or Ouse,
Hence Suffolk dairy-wives run mad for cream,
And leave their milk with nothing but its name;
Its name derision and reproach pursue,
And strangers tell of 'three times skimm'd sky-blue.'
To cheese converted, what can be its boast?
What, but the common virtues of a post!
If drought o'ertake it faster than the knife,
Most fair it bids for stubborn length of life,
And, like the oaken shelf whereon 'tis laid,
Mocks the weak efforts of the bending blade;

Or in the hog-trough rests in perfect spite,
Too big to swallow, and too hard to bite.
Inglorious victory! Ye Cheshire meads,
Or Severn's flow'ry dales, where Plenty treads,
Was your rich milk to suffer wrongs like these,
Farewell your pride! farewell renowned cheese!
The skimmer dread, whose ravages alone
Thus turn the mead's sweet nectar into stone.

ROBERT BLOOMFIELD (1766–1823)

Verses from The Farmer's Boy, *A Rural Poem.*
Bloomfield was born at Honnington in Suffolk.

February 28th, 1785:

. . . The Frost severer than ever in the night
as it even froze the Chamber Pots under the
Beds. Wind very rough and tho' the Sun shone
all the morning very bright yet it continued
freezing every minute. Most bitter cold today
indeed, and likely to continue . . .

THE REVEREND JAMES WOODFORDE (1740–1803)

Woodforde, Rector of Weston Longville, Norfolk, wrote a Diary.

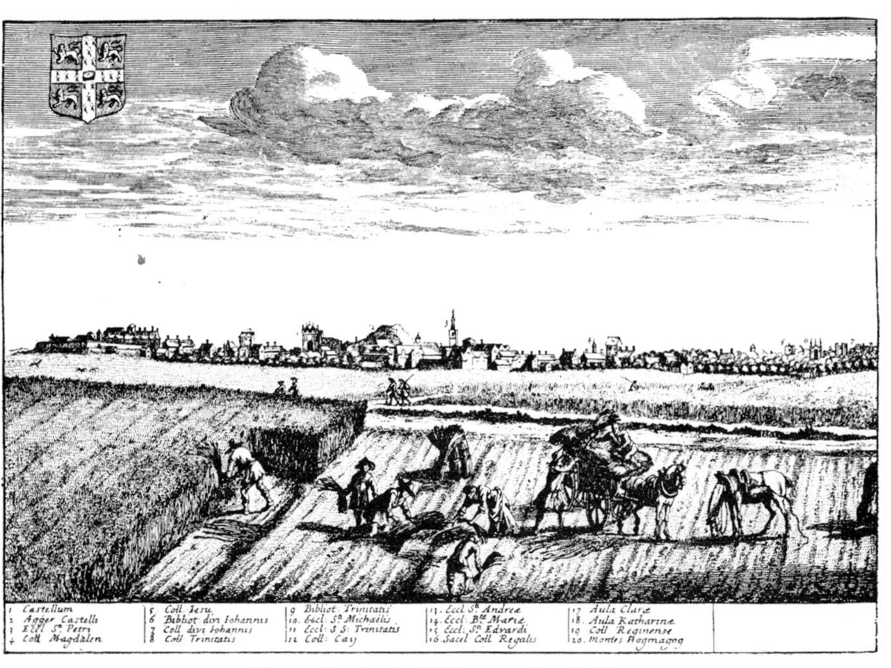

Harvesting in the fields near Cambridge

Why, listen yow—be quiet bo'!—the bell is tolling eight—
Why don't yow mind what yow're about?—We're allers kind o' late!
Now, Mary, get that mawther dressed—oh dear! how slow yow fare—
There come a lot o' gleaners now.—Maw', don't stand gawkin' there!
Now, Janie, goo get that 'ere coach, an' put them pillars in—
Oh! won't I give it yow, my dear, if I do once begin!
Get that 'ere bottle, too—ah, yow may well stand there an' sneer;
What *will* yowr father say, d'ye think, if we don't taak his beer?
Come, Willie!—Jane, where *is* he gone? Goo yow an' fetch that child
If yow don't move them legs of yow'rn, yow'll maak me kind o' riled!
There, lock the door, an' lay the key behind that 'ere old plate;
An' Jemmy, yow run on afore, and ope the whatefeld gate.
Well here we be at last—oh, dear! how fast my heart do beat!
Now, Jane, set yow by this 'ere coach, an' don't yow leave your seat
Till that 'ere precious child's asleep; then bring yow that 'ere sack
An' see if yow can't try today to kin' o' bend your back!
Yow'll all wish, when the winter come, and yow ha'en't got no bread,
That for all drawlin' about so, yow'd harder wrought instead;
For all your father 'arn most goo old Skin'em's rent to pay,
And Mister Last, the shoemaker; so work yow hard, I pray.

* * *

Dear me! there goo the bell agin—'tis seven, I declare;
An' we don't 'pear to have got none;—the gleanin' now don't
fare
To be worth nothin'; but I think—as far as I can tell—
We'll try a coomb, somehow, to scratch, if we be 'live an' well.

'QUILL'
(JOHN IMPIT LUSHINGTON 1830–1881)

The Spiritual Railway

The Line to heaven by Christ was made
With heavenly truth the Rails are laid,
From Earth to Heaven the Line extends,
To Life Eternal where it ends.
Repentance is the Station then
Where Passengers are taken in,
No Fee for them is there to pay,
For Jesus is himself the way.
God's Word is the first Engineer
It points the way to Heaven so clear.
Through tunnels dark and dreary here
It does the way to Glory steer.
God's Love the Fire, his Truth the Steam,
Which drives the Engine and the Train,
All you who would to Glory ride,
Must come to Christ, in him abide
In First, and Second, and Third Class
Repentance, Faith and Holiness,
You must the way to Glory gain
Or you with Christ will not remain.
Come then poor Sinners, now's the time
At any Station on the Line,
If you'll respect and turn from sin
The Train will stop and take you in.

In the Cloister, Ely Cathedral, memorial to W. Pickering and R. Edgar, who died in an 1845 accident on the Norwich to Ely line.

Norfolk

How did the Devil come? When first attack?
   These Norfolk lanes recall lost innocence,
The years fall off and find me walking back
   Dragging a stick along the wooden fence
Down this same path, where, forty years ago,
My father strolled behind me, calm and slow.

I used to fill my hand with sorrel seeds
   And shower him with them from the tops of stiles,
I used to butt my head into his tweeds
   To make him hurry down those languorous miles
Of ash and alder-shaded lanes, till here
Our moorings and the masthead would appear.

There after supper lit by lantern light
   Warm in the cabin I could lie secure
And hear against the polished sides at night
   The lap lap lapping of the weedy Bure,
A whispering and watery Norfolk sound
Telling of all the moonlit reeds around.

How did the Devil come? When first attack?
   The church is just the same, though now I know
Fowler of Louth restored it. Time, bring back
   The rapturous ignorance of long ago,
The peace, before the dreadful daylight starts,
Of unkept promises and broken hearts.

JOHN BETJEMAN (1906–   )

from *Rural Rides*, March 1830

Arrived at Ely, I first walked round the beautiful cathedral, that honour to our Catholic forefathers, and that standing disgrace to our Protestant selves. It is impossible to look at that magnificent pile without *feeling* that we are a fallen race of men. The cathedral would, leaving out the palace of the bishop and the houses of the dean, canons, and prebendaries, weigh more, if it were put into a scale, than all the houses in the town, and all the houses for a mile round the neighbourhood if you exclude the remains of the ancient monasteries. You have only to open your eyes to be convinced that England must have been a far greater and more wealthy country in those days than it is in these days. The hundreds of thousands of loads of stone, of which this cathedral and the monasteries in the neighbourhood were built, must all have been brought by sea from distant parts of the kingdom. These foundations were laid more than a thousand years ago; and yet there are vagabonds who have the impudence to say that it is the Protestant religion that has made England a great country.

WILLIAM COBBETT (1763–1835)

Ely Cathedral, 1837 (South-East View from Barway Bank)

Yuletide in Norfolk

The long-ships drove up the Bure, and the horned men were
there to rape and to burn,
Seeding their names, Rollesby and Billockby, Fleggburgh,
Clippesby and Thurne,
Ashby and Oby. Our church roofs came from the rot of each
oak-warped stern.

But the Nazarene grip was strong. The surge of energy in
the whoring blood
Settled for the purpled moan of the organ, the heifer
chewing her cud,
And the cart with its thwarted axle broken and stuck in
December mud.

I drive to the service at Clippesby, a mile along
sugar-beet-sodden road.
My lights throw up the parishioners, whipped by the
Christian goad
And the hope of Heaven, their faces pinched by a cold,
unearthly woad

Into shapes of bread and wine. Their archangels gloat and
wither on spruce,
Bald winter's fuel from Norway. The tied surplice is
shaken loose,
And the paean rises, the bitter semen of prayer squeezed
like a juice.

Nothing can alter the sounded heritage from the
throbbing brine,
The keels lifting above the waves. Let humility
be divine.
All arrogance is human, the black pride of the Vikings
is mine.

GEORGE MACBETH (1932–)

Ware the Hawk

Prologus Skeltonidis Laureati super Ware the Hawk

THIS work deviséd is
For such as do amiss;
And specially to control
Such as have cure of soul,
That be so far abuséd
They cannot be excuséd
By reason nor by law;
But that they play the daw,
To hawk, or else to hunt
From the altar to the font,
With cry unreverent,
Before the sacrament,
Within holy church's boundés,
That of our faith the ground is.
That priest that hawkés so
All grace is far him fro;
He seemeth a schismatic.
Or else an heretic,
For faith in him is faint.
Therefore to make complaint
Of such misadviséd
Parsons and disguiséd,
This book we have deviséd,
Compendiously compriséd,
No good priest to offend,
But such daws to amend,
In hope that no man shall
Be miscontent withal.

I shall you make relation,
By way of apostrophation,
Under supportation
Of your patient toleration,

How I, Skelton Laureate,
Deviséd and also wrate
Upon a lewd curáte,
A parson beneficéd,
But nothing well adviséd.
He shall be as now nameless,
But he shall not be blameless,
Nor he shall not be shameless;
For sure he wrought amiss
To hawk in my church of Diss.
This fond frantic falconer,
With his polluted pawtener,
As priest unreverent,
Straight to the sacrament
He made his hawk to fly,
With hugeous shout and cry.
The high altar he stripped naked;
Thereon he stood and crakéd;
He shook down all the clothés,
And sware horrible oathés
Before the face of God,
By Moses and Aaron's rod,
Ere that he hence yede
His hawk should pray and feed
Upon a pigeon's maw.
The blood ran down raw
Upon the altar-stone;
The hawk tiréd on a bone;
And in the holy place
She dungéd there a chase
Upon my corporas' face.
Such *sacrificium laudis*
He made with such gambades.

OBSERVATE

His second hawk waxéd gery,
And was with flying weary;
She had flowen so oft,
That on the rood-loft
She perchéd her to rest.
The falconer then was prest,
Came running with a dow,
And cried 'Stow, stow, stow!'
But she would not bow.
He then, to be sure,
Calléd her with a lure.
Her meat was very crude,
She had not well endued;
She was not clean ensaiméd,
She was not well reclaiméd:
But the falconer unfainéd
Was much more feebler brainéd.
The hawk had no list
To come to his fist;
She lookéd as she had the frounce;
With that he gave her a bounce
Full upon the gorge.
I will not feign nor forge—
The hawkė with that clap
Fell down with evil hap.
The church doors were sparréd.
Fast bolted and barréd,
Yet with a pretty gin
I fortuned to come in,
This rebel to behold,
Whereof I him controlled.
But he saidė that he would,
Against my mind and will,
In my church hawkė still.

CONSIDERATE

On Saint John decollation
He hawkéd in this fashion,
Tempore vesperarum.
Sed non secundum Sarum,
But like a March harum
His braines were so *parum.*
He said he would not let
His houndés for to fet,
To hunt there by liberty
In the despite of me,
And to halloo there the fox.
Down went my offering-box,
Book, bell, and candle.
All that he might handle—
Cross, staff, lectern, and banner,
Fell down in this manner.

JOHN SKELTON (1460–1529)

Skelton, the Poet Laureate, was Rector of St. Mary's, Diss. These verses from his poem tell of strange doings in his church.

Epitaph for Mrs Sarah Cargill

Dear Love, one Feather'd minute and I come
To lye down in they darke Retireing Roome
And mingle Dust with thine, that wee may have,
As when alive one Bed, so dead one Grave:
And may my Soul teare through the vaulted Sky
To be with thine to all Eternitie.
O how our Bloudless Formes will that Day greet
With Love Divine when we again shall meet
Devest of all Contagion of the Flesh
Full filled with everlasting joys and Fresh
In Heaven above (and 't may be) cast an eye
How far Elizium doth beaneath us lye.
Deare, I disbody and away
More Swift than Wind
Or Flying Hind
I come I come away.

Mrs Sarah Cargill died in 1680.
The inscription, written by her husband, is in
St. Mary Magdalen Church, Mulbarton,
Norfolk.

On Walsingham

In the wrackes of Walsingham
  Whom should I chuse
But the Queen of Walsingham
  To be guide to my muse?

Then thou Prince of Walsingham
  Grant me to frame
Bitter plaintes to rewe they wrong
  Bitter wo for thy name.

Bitter was it oh to see
  The seely sheepe
Murdered by the raveninge wolves
  While the sheephards did sleep.

Bitter was it oh to vewe
  The sacred vyne
While the gardiners plaied all close
  Rooted up by the swine.

Bitter, bitter oh to behould
  The grasse to growe
Where the walls of Walsingham
  So stately did shewe.

Such were the works of Walsingham
  Where she did stand
Such are the wrackes as noe do shewe
  Of that holy land.

Levell levell with the ground
  The towres doe lye
Which with their golden, glitteringe tops
  Pearsed once to the sky.

Where weare gates no gates are nowe,
 The waies unknowen,
Where the press of peares did pass
 While her fame was far blowen.

Oules do scrike where the sweetest himnes
 Lately were songe,
Toades and serpents hold their dennes
 Where the palmers did throng.

Weepe, weepe O Walsingham,
 Whose dayes are nightes,
Blessings turned to blasphemies,
 Holy deeds to dispites.

Sinne is where our Ladie sate,
 Heaven turned is to hell,
Sathan sittes where our Lord did swaye,
 Walsingham oh farewell.

Attributed to SAINT PHILIP HOWARD,
EARL OF ARUNDEL (1557–1595).

Remains of Walsingham Abbey, 1812

Letter to Saint Peter

Let them in, Peter, they are very tired,
Give them the couches where the angels sleep.
Let them wake whole again to new dawns fired
With sun, not war, and may their peace be deep;
Remember where the broken bodies lie . . .
And give them things they like. Let them make noise,
God knows how young they were to have to die!
Give swing bands, not gold harps, to these our boys.
Let them love, Peter—they had no time—
Girls sweet as meadow wind with flowering hair . . .
They should have trees and bird songs, hills to climb,
The taste of summer in a ripened pear. Tell them
How they are missed. Say not to fear; it's going
To be all right with us down here.

ELMA DEAN

Mrs Dorothea Howlett wife of the former was a very good sort of motherly woman. She was a spirited woman in her youth, and she deceived me until the latter days of her life for on her death bed I had to baptize as well as administer the Sacrament to her. She lamented her negligence. But she was brought up a Dissenter, and taught in my school the Church Catechism &c. &c., and only in her decline confessed to me that she herself had never been admitted through Baptism into the Covenant of Christ's Church. She had been taught that Christ being baptised was all-sufficient.

I never had any occasion to find fault with her attention to the girls under her care. She taught needlework and reading and spelling very well, but she shocked me greatly when she told me of the years of hypocracy which she had spent.

THE REVEREND RICHARD COBBOLD (1797–1877)

Cobbold was Rector of this Suffolk village for many years.

There was a young lady of Lynn
Who was deep in original sin;
  When they said, 'Do be good!'
  She said, 'Would if I could!'
And straightway went at it again.

?ANON.

Epitaph for Anna Maria Vassa

Near this Place lies Interred
ANNA MARIA VASSA
Daughter of GUSTAVUS VASSA the AFRICAN
She died July 21 1797
Aged 4 years

Should simple village rhymes attract thine eye,
Stranger, as thoughtfully you passest by,
Know that there lies beside this humble stone
A child of colour haply not thine own.
Her father born of Afric's sun-burnt race,
Torn from his native fields, ah foul disgrace:
Through various toils, at length to Britain came
Espous'd, so Heaven ordain'd, an English dame,
And followed Christ: their hope two infants dear.
But one, a hapless Orphan, slumbers here,
To bury her the village children came
And dropp'd choice flowers, and lisp'd her early fame:
And some that loved her most as if unblest
Bedew'd with tears the white wreath on their breast:
But she is gone and dwells in that abode
Where some of every clime shall joy in God.

From a tombstone in Chesterton churchyard
near Cambridge.

Ely is in the province of the East Angles, a country of about six hundred families, in the nature of an island, enclosed, as has been said, either with marshes or waters, and therefore it has its name from the great plenty of eels taken in those marshes; there the aforesaid servant of Christ desired to have a monastery, because, as we have before observed, she was descended from that same province of the East Angles.

I think it proper to insert in this history a hymn of virginity, which I composed in elegiac verse several years ago, in praise and honour of the same queen and spouse of Christ; and to imitate the method of the Holy Scripture, in whose history many poetical pieces are inserted which are known to be composed in metre.

> . . . Thus Etheldrida, pure from sensual crime,
> British shining star! arose to bless our time.
> Born of a regal race, her sire a king,
> More noble honour to her lord shall bring.
> A queen her name, her hand a sceptre rears,
> But greater glories wait above the spheres.
> What man wouldst thou desire? See Christ is made
> Her spouse, her blessed Redeemer weds the maid.
> While you attend the heavenly Mother's train,
> Thou shalt be mother of a heavenly reign.
> The holy maid who twelve years sat a queen,
> A cloistered nun devote to God was seen.
> Noted for pious deeds, her spotless soul
> Left the vile world, and soar'd above the pole.
> Sixteen Novembers since was the blest maid
> Entomb'd, whose flesh no putrid damps invade.
> No tainted vest wrapping the corpse around.
> The swelling dropsy, and dire atrophy,
> A pale disease from the blest vestments fly.
> Rags fires the fiend, who whilom Eve betray'd,
> While shouting angels hail the glorious maid.
> See! wedded to her God, what joy remains,

In earth, or heaven, see! with her God she reigns!
Behold! the spouse, the festal torches shine,
He comes! behold! what joyful gifts are thine!
Thou a new song on the sweet harp shall sing,
A hymn of praise to thy celestial King.
None from the flock of the throned Lamb shall move,
Whom grateful passion bind, and heavenly love.

Bede (673–735)

Saint Etheldrida (c. 630–679), Abbess and foundress of the Benedictine house of Ely, was daughter of King Anna of the East Angles. This account of her is from The Ecclesiastical History of the English Nation *by Bede, who was a monk at Jarrow.*

Our Lady of Walsingham

There once the penitents took off their shoes
And then walked barefoot the remaining mile;
And the small trees, a stream and hedgerows file
Slowly along the munching English lane,
Like cows to the old shrine, until you lose
Track of your dragging pain.
The stream flows down under the druid tree,
Shiloah's whirlpools gurgle and make glad
The castle of God. Sailor, you were glad
And whistled Sion by that stream. But see:

Our Lady, too small for her canopy,
Sits near the altar. There's no comeliness
At all or charm in that expressionless
Face with its heavy eyelids. As before,
This face, for centuries a memory,
Non est species, neque decor.
Expressionless, expresses God: it goes
Past castled Sion. She knows what God knows,
Not Calvary's Cross nor crib at Bethlehem
Now, and the world shall come to Walsingham.

ROBERT LOWELL (1917–1977)

I remember well that, when I was preparing . . . I had such an idea I should undergo an examination and I was so fearful of some wry question that might discountenance me, that I learnt nearly the whole common prayer book by heart!—Besides reading the Bible quite through three times! I was so indefatigable, I rose to nothing else; and never went to rest while I could procure light for my labours. Alex would not be much led to imitate me, if he knew that, after all this hard work—the fat clumsy stumpy worthy Bishop of Norwich clapt his hand upon my head, and off it, as fast as he possibly could, and never made a single interrogatory, nor uttered a single doubt or demur upon my fitness or unfitness for his blessing.

FANNY BURNEY (1752–1840)

The novelist, born at King's Lynn, Norfolk, recalling her confirmation when, many years later, she was preparing her son for his.

Holkham Hall

Where Holkham rears in graceful pride
  Her marble halls and crested towers,
And stretches o'er the champaign wide
  Her lengthened suite of social bowers;

Where, led by Leicester's forming hand,
  To Nature Art her succour gives,
Touches the desert with her wand,
  And sculpture breathes and painting lives;

Sheltered beneath this friendly dome,
  Far from the world's tumultuous rage,
I ope the venerated tome,
  And read, and glow along the page.

* * *

But happier far the moments fly
  When, resting from my lengthened toil,
I meet with Coke's benignant eye,
  And share his kind approving smile;

Friend of his country and mankind,
  To more than titled honours born;
Who looks with independent mind
  On all the venal tribes with scorn.

His the firm soul to freedom true,
  The open heart, the liberal hand
That from the rock the waters drew,
  And bade the bounteous stream expand,

To clothe the plain with brighter green,
  The soil with richer harvests bless,
And pour on all the cultured scene
  The glow of life and happiness:

Not with scant hand the pittance small
 To starving industry to give;
But grant their general rights to all,
 And as he lives, let others live.

And sees, with all a parent's pride,
 His healthful village train display'd,
To heal the wounds in nature's side,
 By tyrants and by heroes made.

WILLIAM ROSCOE (1753–1831)

Roscoe was for a time Librarian in the Great Library of the famous Coke of Norfolk at Holkham Hall.

It is a melancholy thing to stand alone
in one's own country. I look around,
not a house to be seen but my own. I am
Giant of Giant Castle, and have ate up
all my neighbours—my nearest neighbour
is the King of Denmark.

SIR THOMAS COKE (1697–1759)

Coke, for whom Holkham Hall, Norfolk, was built, was created Earl of Leicester in 1744.

Holkham Hall, visited by the Prince and Princess of Wales, 1865.

March 25th, 1761:

. . . Here I am at Houghton! and alone! in this spot where I have not been in sixteen years! Think what a crowd of reflections!—no Gray, and forty churchyards, could not furbish so many: nay, I know one must feel them with greater indifference than I possess, to have patience to put them into verse. Here I am, probably for the last time of my life, though not for the last time—every clock that strikes tells me I am an hour nearer to yonder church—that church, into which I have not had courage to enter, where lies that Mother on whom I doted, and who doted on me! There are the two rival mistresses of Houghton, neither of whom wished to enjoy it! There too lies he who founded its greatness, to contribute to whose fall Europe was embroiled—there he sleeps in quiet and dignity, until his friend and foe, rather his false ally and real enemy, Newcastle and Bath, are exhausting the dregs of their pitiful lives in squabbles and pamphlets!

The surprise the pictures gave me is again renewed—accustomed for many years to see nothing but wretched daubs and varnished copies at auctions, I look at these as enchantment . . . A party arrived, just as I did, to see the house, a man and three women in riding dresses and they rode post through the appartments—I could not hurry before them fast enough—they were not so long in *seeing* for the first time, as I could have been in one room, to examine what I knew by heart. I remember formerly being often diverted with this kind of seers—they come, ask what such a room is called, in which Sir Robert lay, write it down, admire a lobster or a cabbage in a market place, dispute whether the last room was green or purple, then hurry to the inn for fear the fish should be over-dressed . . .

HORACE WALPOLE (1717–1797)

From a letter to George Montagu.

January 28th, 1780:

. . . The company present were Sir Edmund Bacon and Lady, Mr and Mrs Custance and Mr Press Custance . . . We had for dinner a Calf's Head, boiled Fowl and Tongue, a Saddle of Mutton rosted on the Side Table, and a fine Swan rosted with Currant Jelly for the First Course. The Second Course a couple of Wild Fowl called Dun Fowls, Larks, Blamange, Tarts etc etc and a good Dessert of Fruit after, amongst which was a Damson Cheese. I never eat a bit of Swan before, and I think it good eating with sweet sauce . . .

THE REVEREND JAMES WOODFORDE
(1740–1803)

Little Peggy

My noble, lovely, little Peggy,
Let this my first epistle beg ye
At dawn of morn and close of even
To lift your heart and hands to Heaven.
In double beauty say your prayer,
Our Father first, and then *nôtre Père*,
And, dearest child, along the day,
In everything you do or say
Obey and please my Lord and Lady,
So God shall love, and angels aid ye.

If to these precepts you attend,
No second letter need I send:
And so I rest your constant friend.

MATTHEW PRIOR (1664–1721)

Prior wrote these lines in 1720 to the child heiress of his patron, the Earl of Oxford, at Wimpole Hall, Cambridgeshire.

[A man] in a Morrice keepe mee company to Bury: I being glad of his friendly offer, gaue him thankes, and forward wee did set: but ere euer wee had measur'd halfe a mile of our way, he gaue me ouer in the plain field, protesting, that if he might get a 100. pound, he would not hold out with me; for indeed my pace in dauncing is not ordinary.

As he and I were parting, a lusty Country lasse being among the people, cal'd him faint hearted lout: saying, if I had begun to daunce, I would haue held out one myle though it had cost my life. At which wordes many laughed. Nay saith she, if the Dauncer will lend me a leash of his belles, Ile venter to treade one mile with him my selfe. I lookt vpon her, saw mirth in her eies, heard boldnes in her words, and beheld her ready to tucke vp her russet petticoate, I fitted her with bels: which she merrily taking, garnisht her thicke short legs, and with a smooth brow bad the Tabrer begin. The Drum strucke, forward marcht I with my merry Maydemarian: who shooke her fat sides: and footed it merrily to Melfoord, being a long myle. There parting with her, I gaue her (besides her skinfull of drinke) an English crowne to buy more drinke, for good wench she was in a pittious heate: my kindnes she requited with dropping some dozen of short courtsies, and bidding God blesse the Dauncer, I bad her adiue: and to giue her her due, she had a good eare, daunst truely, and wee parted friendly. But ere I part with her, a good fellow my friend, hauin writ an odde Rime of her, I will make bolde to set it downe.

A Country Lasse browne as a berry,
Blith of blee in heart as merry,
Cheekes well fed and sides well larded,
Euery bone with fat flesh guarded,
Meeting merry Kemp by chaunce,
Was Marrian in his Morrice daunce.
Her stump legs with bels were garnisht,
Her browne browes with sweating varnish;
Her browne hips when she was lag,
To win her ground, went swig a swag,
Which to see all that came after,

Were repleate with mirthfull laughter.
Yet she thumpt it on her way,
With a sportly hey de gay,
At a mile her daunce she ended,
Kindly paide and well commended.

At Melford, diuers Gentlemen met mee, who brought me to one master Colts, a very kinde and worshipfull Gentleman, where I had vnexpected entertainment till the Satterday. From whose house hauing hope somewhat to amend my way to Bury, I determined to goe by Clare, but I found it to be both farther and fouler.

WILL KEMP (*fl.* 1600)

This account of his jig for a bet from London to Norwich by Kemp, one of the clowns in Shakespeare's acting Company, was published in 1600.

Powte's Complaint

Come, Brethren of the water, and let us all assemble,
To treat upon this matter, which makes us quake and tremble;
For we shall rue it, if 't be true, that Fens be undertaken,
And where we feed in Fen and Reed, they'll feed both Beef and Bacon

They'll sow both beans and oats, where never man yet thought it,
Where men did row in boats, ere undertakers bought it:
But, Ceres, thou, behold us now, let wild oats be their venture,
Oh let the frogs and miry bogs destroy where they do enter.

Behold the great design, which they do now determine,
Will make our bodies pine, a prey to crows and vermine:
For they do mean all Fens to drain, and waters overmaster,
All will be dry, and we must die, 'cause Essex calves want pasture.

Away with boats and rudder, farewell both boots and skatches,
No need of one nor th'other, men now make better matches;
Stilt-makers all and tanners, shall complain of this disaster,
For they will make each muddy lake for Essex calves a pasture.

The feather'd fowls have wings, to fly to other nations;
But we have no such things, to help our transportations;
We must give place (oh grievous case) to horned beasts and cattle,
Except that we can all agree to drive them out by battle.

ANON.

Verses from a seventeenth-century song against the Fen draining schemes. A 'powte' is a sea-lamprey.

PART I: WINTER 1618

EVENSONG

'Christ is your King.' Jesse Sease, the preacher,
 says that, lifting one hand
and flooding our narrow church with shadow:
 'He gave you this land.'

I watch his shadows, trying to enter their darkness;
 they flicker on stone, then pass
over rows of sloped necks into the stiff folds
 of saints strolling in glass.

There is no comfort here, only a long absence
 where I exercise rage;
the real King is nearer, last night
 his men harassed the village,

mapping our fresh springs, describing our fields
 with their lamps.
Soon they will come again; already perspectives
 shift under the stamp

of their will. Until then, as I look up,
 the place returns to me:
God's unfinished landscape, an empty marsh,
 the sun dissolving light in the North Sea.

A VIEW FROM THE PORCH

I grew up here, I know
how to possess the place;
its watery secrets, its slow
gestation of sinuous roots
will go if I go.

We built this wall to keep
tides from it. We thought life
transferred from hands to the steep
rim of our world would define
our claim, secure us the easy sleep

of rightful inheritors. But still
the tides come in, slithering
over the wall each winter until
they cancel our ditches, drown
the crops on our low hills.

Under their swell, the wall's strong
unbroken wake always survives;
now I will imitate where I belong,
—that white arm lining the bay
limits the hope I live among.

WALKING HOME

Someone is playing a flute as I walk home
    by the wall; the notes
tauten on miles of blue, feathery marsh, then break
    across estuaries, boats,

and into the flat sea. Hung round the bay,
   houses look down to it,
occasional bleached walls twisting a lamplight
   out through a slit,

most abandoned. The notes repeat and repeat
   over smashed beams,
a drift of tinkling dust, rephrasing
   their dispossessed dreams.

So many have left already, their rooms
   darkened again
by strangers completing the King's command:
   what remains

is only their echo returning to silence,
   and us, lingering here
ensnared by memory; pride;
   fear.

HOME

Wind shakes the door.
Love, kneel by me here
at the fire, before
its warmth fails. Darkness
has smothered the sea's roar,

and even the strangers
sleep in their rough camps;
now while the globe blurs
take my life in your hands
out of all danger.

Shadow falls from your face
into the red flames; let it
lie there, until each trace
of the present burns, and we
are without place.

Tomorrow, high tides will press
our future from us
back into emptiness;
so now, unpin your hair,
open your dress.

HIGH TIDE

A bar of moonlight tilts beyond the head,
melts underwater, then trawls in
the tide towards us on a liquid thread.
Early ripples smear against the wall.

Out there, the sea
reflects its planet's flawless steps
—element with element in sympathy
obliterating margins round the bay.

The marsh contracts beneath their weight,
its channels reeled uphill
as hour by hour the breakers grate
closer through deserted lanes

until the farmlights gleam like ships
and running shadows wash across our room.
Look: below the window, contours slip,
unravelled between waves and light;

a gauze of slime has trailed above
the low wall at the estuary,
and fields must open to the water's shove
where fish already strain inland.

ANDREW MOTION (1952–   )

These are the opening verses of his poem, which won the Newdigate Prize. The poem speaks of seventeenth-century Fenland enclosures.

They hang the man and flog the woman
Who steals the goose from off the Common;
But let the greater criminal loose
Who steals the Common from the goose.

An anonymous view of the enclosures in Suffolk

from *The Dawn in Britain*

Night on East hills now is the dawn to rise . . .
Then spake Boudicca . . .
  'Shall all one wreak, one ruin overtake
Them, impious bondslaves of incestuous Caesar;
Whose Roman crimes unheard, since the world was!
For Nero, in his hell-fury, entered in
Womb that conceived, of his thrice-cursed dam,
That bare him; his own mother knew! What then?
He murdered her! bade rip her belly then: . . .
Tread down, O Britons, cinders of your hearths!'
  Boudicca Queen, thus saying let backward slide
Unto the girle-stead, her shining weed;
But seemly gathered, stern, before her breast,
And all deformed that angry multitude
Beheld, with Catus' scourges and vile rods,
Chine of the widow of royal Prasutagos!
How long, Boudicca weeps, great saviour goddess,
Chaste Brigit, guardian of our sacred hearth! . . .

CHARLES DOUGHTY (1843–1926)

Doughty, the author of Travels in Arabia Deserta, *was born in Suffolk. Boudicca was Queen of the Iceni, a powerful East Anglian people.*

from *An Horatian Ode upon Cromwell's Return from Ireland*

So restless *Cromwel* could not cease
In the inglorious Arts of Peace,
  But through adventrous War
  Urged his active Star.
And, like the three-fork'd Lightning, first
Breaking the Clouds where it was nurst,
  Did thorough his own Side
  His fiery way divide.
For 'tis all one to Courage high
The Emulous or Enemy;
  And with such to inclose
  Is more than to oppose.
Then burning through the Air he went,
And Pallaces and Temples rent:
  And *Caesars* head at last
  Did through his Laurels blast.
'Tis Madness to resist or blame
The force of angry Heavens flame:
  And, if we would speak true,
  Much to the Man is due.
Who, from his private Gardens, where
He liv'd reserved and austere,
  As if his highest plot
  To plant the Bergamot,
Could by industrious Valour climbe
To ruine the great Work of Time,
  And cast the Kingdome old
  Into another Mold.
Though Justice against Fate complain,
And plead the antient Rights in vain:
  But those do hold or break
  As Men are strong or weak.
Nature that hateth emptiness,
Allows of penetration less:
  And therefore must make room

Where greater Spirits come.
What Field of all the Civil Wars,
Where his were not the deepest Scars?

ANDREW MARVELL (1621–1678)

Cromwell was born in Huntingdon.

Tom Paine

In digging up your bones, Tom Paine,
Will Cobbett has done well;
You visit him on earth again,
He'll visit you in hell.

LORD BYRON (1788–1824)

Tom Paine (1737–1809), the revolutionary, was born in Thetford. Cobbett wanted to bring his bones from America and give him a burial in England.

On Lady Katherine Paston's Tomb at Oxnead

Sun set three hundred years,
These marble shadows on the wall still stand,
Fixed by her husband's grief, and Stone's hand,
Long vanished skill, and wealth, and tears.

Outside her dilapidated
Church the usual June again transposes
The graveyard offals into grass and roses,
Beauty and corruption equated,

Balanced principles,
Whereby this white memento-mori is
Now mere memoria pulchritudinis,
New summer dappling her walls.

We're not the tomorrow, alas,
Of this lady's wish; her treasures scattered for ever,
Her mansion now green mounds beside the river,
Not a Paston left to wear her flesh . . .

And since we put the resurrection
Even of annual crops to chance,
Eternity of blood's no longer, as once,
Any man's confident possession.

We do with less than that:
The uncertain hope that someone not yet born
May saunter here on a remote June morning
To find the key under the mat.

MICHAEL RIVIERE (1919–)

Boadicea, an Ode

When the British warrior queen,
Bleeding from the Roman rods,
Sought with an indignant mien,
Counsel of her country's gods,

Sage beneath a spreading oak
Sat the Druid, hoary chief,
Ev'ry burning word he spoke,
Full of rage and full of grief.

Princess! if our aged eyes
Weep upon thy matchless wrongs,
'Tis because resentment ties
All the terrors of our tongues.

Rome shall perish—write that word
In the blood that she has spilt;
Perish hopeless and abhorr'd,
Deep in ruin as in guilt.

Rome for empire far renown'd,
Tramples on a thousand states,
Soon her pride shall kiss the ground--
Hark! the Gaul is at her gates.

Other Romans shall arise,
Heedless of a soldier's name,
Sounds, not arms, shall win the prize,
Harmony the path to fame.

Then the progeny that springs
From the forests of our land,
Arm'd with thunder, clad with wings,
Shall a wider world command.

Regions Caesar never knew,
   Thy posterity shall sway,
Where his eagles never flew,
   None invincible as they.

Such the bard's prophetic words,
   Pregnant with celestial fire,
Bending as he swept the chords
   Of his sweet but awful lyre.

She with all a monarch's pride,
   Felt them in her bosom glow,
Rush'd to battle, fought and died,
   Dying, hurl'd them at the foe.

Ruffians, pittiless as proud,
   Heav'n awards the vengeance due,
Empire is on us bestow'd,
   Shame and ruin wait for you.

William Cowper (1731–1800)

from *The Miller's Daughter*

Then leapt a trout. In lazy mood
  I watch'd the little circles die;
They past into the level flood,
  And there a vision caught my eye;
The reflex of a beauteous form,
  A glowing arm, a gleaming neck,
As when a sunbeam wavers warm
  Within the dark and dimpled beck.

For you remember, you had set,
  That morning, on the casement's edge
A long green box of mignonette,
  And you were leaning from the ledge:
And when I raised my eyes, above
  They met with two so full and bright—
Such eyes! I swear to you, my love,
  That these have never lost their light.

I loved, and love dispell'd the fear
  That I should die an early death:
For love possess'd the atmosphere,
  And fill'd the breast with purer breath,
My mother thought, What ails the boy?
  For I was alter'd, and began
To move about the house with joy,
  And with the certain step of man.

I loved the brimming wave that swam
  Thro' quiet meadows round the mill,
The sleepy pool above the dam,
  The pool beneath it never still,
The meal-sacks on the whiten'd floor,
  The dark round of the dripping wheel,
The very air about the door
  Made misty with the floating meal.

* * *

Ah, well—but sing the foolish song
  I gave you, Alice, on the day
When, arm in arm, we went along,
  A pensive pair, and you were gay
With bridal flowers—that I may seem,
  As in the nights of old, to lie
Beside the mill-wheel in the stream,
  While those full chestnuts whisper by.

It is the miller's daughter,
  And she is grown so dear, so dear,
That I would be the jewel
  That trembles at her ear:
For hid in ringlets day and night,
I'd touch her neck so warm and white.

And I would be the girdle
  About her dainty dainty waist,
And her heart would beat against me,
  In sorrow and in rest:
And I should know if it beat right,
I'd clasp it round so close and tight.

And I would be the necklace,
  And all day long to fall and rise
Upon her balmy bosom,
  With her laughter or her sighs,
And I would lie so light, so light,
I scarce should be unclasp'd at night.

ALFRED, LORD TENNYSON (1809–1892)

The mill is thought to have been that at Trumpington, Cambridgeshire.

King's Lynn (c. 1700)

King's Lynn

Just opposite the elegant Custom House
So feasibly attributed to Wren
We watched the racketting pile-driver
Man-shouldered into place
By greasy caps and coats with pennant linings
Fluttering heraldic in the north-east wind.

Beside it on the quay a square-hewn stake
Extracted from the past—a broken tooth
Stained at the root—the crude support
Of civic splendour in the years of grace.

Explore now, as a freak tide might explore
This town that history could have made a city,
Swirl round the leaning pillars of this church
That could be a cathedral, then move on,
Inquisitive as water,
Over the docks, across the squares,
Into courtyards, under entrances.

Leave tides below, and climb
The winding centuries of a merchant's watchtower
To scan the wide way to the wider sea
For pennants fluttering in the north-east wind.

Step down to what the tides have left behind:
In the marsh-sunken chapel-of-ease
Two Dutch-scrubbed likenesses,
A merchant and his wife, as shrewd
And thrifty as the north-east wind,
Square-hewn,
Embedded in the local mud—essential
Supporters of armorial elegance.

R. N. CURREY (1907–)

from *Notes on the Natural History of Norfolk*

A kind of stork was shott in the wing by the sea neere Hasburrowe and brought alive unto mee; it was about a yard high, red head, colourd leggs, and bill, the clawes resembling human nayles, such as Herodotus describeth in the white Ibis of Ægypt. The Lower parts of the wings are black, which gathered up makes the lower part of back looke black, butt the tayle under them is white as the other part of the body. It fed readily upon snayles and froggs, butt a toad being offered it would not touch it: the tongue very short not an inch longe. It makes a clattering noyse by flapping one bill agaynst the other, somewhat like the *platea* or shovelard. The quills of the bignesse of swans bills. When it swallowed a frogge it was sent downe into the stomak by the backside of the neck, as was perceaved upon swallowing. I could not butt take notice of the conceit of some who looked upon it as an ill omen, saying if storks come over into England, pray God a commonwealth do not come after.

* * *

Of Herring incredible shoales passe by this coast about 7tember untill towards the end of October when their shoals move more southward. Unto this fishing boats resort from the north & west country, from the Low Countries & some from France wh. bring in herrings into Yarmouth. Such store sometimes is taken in a day that . . ., that is, above an herring for every man in England. Tis observed that in an east or northeast wind they grow shotten, butt the wind changing in a day or 2 grow full agayne. In their descent from the north they passe not into the bay of Lyne or the south shoare of Norfolk, butt passe beyond the poynt of Cromer. Nothing is found in their bellies, & dye immediately out of the water. The greatest part being salted & hang upon sticks in howses for the purpose & so gently smoake & dryed by a greate furnace especiall of Ash . . . & smoking in a close . . . with the vent at distance from them. This citty is obliged by charter to send unto his Majestie yearly Herring pyes; each contains 3 herrings wch is yearly duly observed.

SIR THOMAS BROWNE (1605–1682)

This author and physician settled in Norwich.

There was a fat lady from Eye
Who felt she was likely to die;
  But for fear that once dead
  She would not be well-fed
She gulped down a pig, a cow, a sheep, twelve
  buns, a seven-layer cake, four cups
  of coffee, and a green apple pie.

?ANON.

Harvest Festivals

a Suffolk expression for a large pair of
knickers: ie 'all gathered in'

TRADITIONAL

Beautiful Technical Language

The north wind blows with gale force.
Sun and moon are convergent.
Tidal phase is at 'high water springs'.
A storm wave has built up by the Shetlands.
Seeking relief, the waters surge southwards.
Along the East Coast they burst over banks,
brim across roads and marshes.
Traffic is halted, houses inundated.
In low-lying Netherlands people drown.
(This we learned later from the papers.)
Before the water can subside
the wind must diminish and change direction,
the moon move in phase
and barometric pressure rise.
All this you explained in
beautiful technical language.

We were together in the hut by the estuary.
A miracle! In the night our world had changed.
We awoke to find water around and beneath us,
for the hut was on stilts.
Two days we were marooned together.
I was not alarmed, alone together.
You said our love was at flood—
had welled to 'high water springs'—
emotion was held in a standing wave—
this came from within,
it could not subside,
there would be no ebb—
we were in phase, convergent,
impervious to ambient conditions.
All this you explained in
beautiful technical language.

The moon since then has opened and shut many times;
has had many phases.
The sea is here.
It lies far below, seen but disregarded.
Where I am, high on the urban cliff top,
wet asphalt gleams dully in the rain.
Buses roll and tilt as they squelch into gutters.
Announcements declare rooms are vacant—but not for us.
Bingo Hall—Sam's Café—a fun place called 'High Jinks'.
Somewhere, a hundred feet or more
below this high-rise block,
the sea lies, disregarded.
The waters do not rise here.
No surges.
Nothing to be explained in
beautiful technical language.

STEPHEN MEADOWS (1904–   )

The Prayse of the Red Herring

A Fisherman of Yarmouth, hauing drawne so many herrings hee wist not what to do withall, hung the residue that he could not sel nor spēd, in the sooty roofe of his shad a drying: or say thus, his shad was a cabbinet in *decimo sexto*, builded on foure crutches, and hee had no roome in it, but in that garret or *Excelsis*, to lodge them, where if they were drie, let them bee drie, for in the sea they had drunke too much, and now hee would force them doo penance for it.

The weather was colde, and good fires hee kept, (as fishermen, what hardnesse soeuer they endure at sea, they will make all smoake, but they will make amendes for it, when they come to land,) and what with his fiering and smoking, or smokie firing, in that his narrow lobby, his herrings, which were as white as whales bone when hee hung them vp, nowe lookt as red as a lobster. It was foure or fiue dayes before either hee or his wife espied it, & when they espied it, they fell downe on their knees & blessed themselus, & cride, a miracle, a miracle & with the proclaiming it among their neighbours they could not be content, but to the court the fisherman would, and present it to the King, then lying at *Burrough* Castle two mile off . . . Saint Denis for Fraunce, Saint James for Spaine, Saint Patrick for Ireland, Saint George for England, and the red Herring for Yarmouth.

THOMAS NASHE (1567–1601)

Nashe was born in Lowestoft, Suffolk.

Thetford

The poets, one and all, were wont to choose
Some fabled, fav'rite Goddess, as their muse.
But gratitude alone my mind inspires,
No other Muse my simple pen requires.
When erst in youth's gay prime and uncontrolled
O Thetford! round thy flow'ry fields I've strolled,
From Tutt-Hill's eminence and Croxton's height,
Have view'd thine ancient ruins with delight,
Thy sloping hills and wooded vallies gay,
Whose silv'ry Ouse meand'ring winds his way.
Though then, each lofty mound, each ruin'd tower,
Told but of war, and time's destructive power;
And thou, they pristine grandeur long had'st lost,
Nor more of Kings, or mighty chiefs could boast;
Yet heartfelt joys beneath they roots I found,
And peace, with all the social blessings crown'd.
To tune his reed, and sing they healing streams,
Then enter'd not the Bard's enraptur'd dreams,
But now the Muse exultingly may sing,
The well attested virtues of thy Spring;
Since erudition and clear truth unite
To chase all fear, and set the judgment right.

George Bloomfield (1757–1831)

The carrier's horse was the laziest horse in the world, I should hope, and shuffled along, with his head down, as if he liked to keep people waiting to whom the packages were directed. I fancied, indeed, that he sometimes chuckled audibly over this reflection, but the carrier said he was only troubled with a cough.

The carrier had a way of keeping his head down, like his horse, and of drooping sleepily forward as he drove, with one of his arms on each of his knees. I say 'drove,' but it struck me that the cart would have gone to Yarmouth quite as well without him, for the horse did all that; and as to conversation, he had no idea of it but whistling.

Peggotty had a basket of refreshments on her knee, which would have lasted us out handsomely, if we had been going to London by the same conveyance. We ate a good deal, and slept a good deal. Peggotty always went to sleep with her chin upon the handle of the basket, her hold of which never relaxed; and I could not have believed unless I had heard her do it, that one defenceless woman could have snored so much.

We made so many deviations up and down lanes, and were such a long time delivering a bedstead at a public-house, and calling at other places, that I was quite tired, and very glad, when we saw Yarmouth. It looked rather spongy and soppy, I thought, as I carried my eye over the great dull waste that lay across the river; and I could not help wondering, if the world were really as round as my geography-book said, how any part of it came to be so flat. But I reflected that Yarmouth might be situated at one of the poles; which would account for it.

As we drew a little nearer, and saw the whole adjacent prospect lying a straight low line under the sky, I hinted to Peggotty that a mound or so might have improved it; and also that if the land had been a little more separated from the sea, and the town and the tide had not been quite so much mixed up, like toast and water, it would have been nicer. But Peggotty said, with greater emphasis than usual, that we must take things as we found them, and that, for her part, she was proud to call herself a Yarmouth Bloater.

When we got into the street (which was strange enough to me), and smelt the fish, and pitch, and oakum, and tar, and saw the sailors walking about, and the carts jingling up and down over the stones, I felt that I had done so busy a place an injustice; and said as much to Peggotty, who heard my expressions of delight with great complacency, and told me it was well known (I suppose to those who had the good fortune to be born Bloaters) that Yarmouth was, upon the whole, the finest place in the universe.

CHARLES DICKENS (1812–1870)

Yarmouth Old Pier

The Waveney

Listen to me—
There is a little river, fed by rills
That winds among the hills,
And turns and suns itself unceasingly,
And wanders through the cornfields wooingly,
For it has nothing else to do, but play
Along its cheery way:
Not like great rivers that in locks are bound,
On whom hard man doth heavy burdens lay,
And fret their waters into foam and spray.
This river's life is one long holiday
All the year round.
Listen and long—
It hears the bells of many churches chime,
It has a pleasant time:
The trees that bow to it their branches strong,
Hide many birds that make its spring one song,
And orchard boughs let fall their flowery wealth,
To float away by stealth,
And land in tiny coves a mile below,
Or round and round the stems of rushes veer
Like snowy foam, but truly none is here,
So calmly gurgle on the waters clear
With endless flow.

JEAN INGELOW (1820–1897)

January 15th, 1908:

Oh Dunwich is beautiful. I am on a heaving moor of heather and close gorse up and down and ending in a sandy cliff about 80 feet perpendicular and the black, peat-strewn fine sand below. On the edge of this 1½ miles away is the ruined church that has half fallen over already. Four arches and a broken tower, pale and airy. Just beyond that the higher moor dips to quite flat marsh with gentlest rises inland with masses of trees compact and dark and a perfect huge curve of foamy coast up to the red light at Southwold northward. In the other direction, just behind us, the moor dips to more marshes with black cattle dim and far off under white sun, and three faint windmills that work a sluice and then trees—inland more gentle rises with pines. No hills (unless you lie down in a dip of the moor and fancy the moorland as part of a Welsh 'black mountain').

EDWARD THOMAS (1878–1917)

From a letter to Gordon Bottomley.

The Flitting

Ive left my own old home of homes
Green fields and every pleasant place
The summer like a stranger comes
I pause and hardly know her face
I miss the hazels happy green
The blue bells quiet hanging blooms
Where envy's sneer was never seen
Where staring malice never comes

I miss the heath its yellow furze
Molehills and rabbit tracks that lead
Through beesom ling and teazel burrs
That spread a wilderness indeed
The woodland oaks and all below
That their white powdered branches shield
The mossy pads—the very crow
Croaked music in my native fields

I sit me in my corner chair
That seems to feel itself from home
I hear bird music here and there
From hawthorn hedge and orchard come
I hear but all is strange and new
—I sat on my old bench in June
The sailing puddocks shrill 'peelew'
Oer royce wood seemed a sweeter tune

I walk adown the narrow lane
The nightingale is singing now
But like to me she seems at loss
For royce wood and its shielding bough
I lean upon the window sill
The trees and summer happy seem
Green sunny green they shine—but still
My heart goes far away to dream

Of happiness and thoughts arise
With home bred pictures many a one
Green lanes that shut out burning skies
And old crooked stiles to rest upon
Above them hangs the maple tree
Below grass swells a velvet hill
And little footpads sweet to see
Goes seeking sweeter places still

With bye and bye a brook to cross
Oer which a little arch is thrown
No brook is here I feel the loss
From home and friends and all alone
—The stone pit with its shelving sides
Seemed hanging rocks in my esteem
I miss the prospect far and wide
From Langley bush and so I seem

Alone and in a stranger scene
Far from spots my heart esteems
The closen with their ancient green
Heath woods and pastures sunny streams
The hawthorns here were hung with may
But still they seem in deader green
The sun een seems to lose its way
Nor knows the quarter it is in

I dwell on trifles like a child
I feel as ill becomes a man
And still my thoughts like weedlings wild
Grow up to blossom where they can
They turn to places known so long
And feel that joy was dwelling there
So homebred pleasure fills the song
That has no present joys to heir

JOHN CLARE (1793–1864)

These are the opening verses of Clare's long lament, when he had to move from his home at Helpston, near Peterborough, Cambridgeshire, to Northborough in the same county.

On planting at the head of FitzGerald's grave two rose-trees whose ancestors had scattered their petals over the tomb of Omar Khayyàm.

'My tomb shall be on a spot where the north wind may strow roses upon it.'

OMAR KHAYYÀM TO KWÁJAH NIZAMI.

Hear us, ye winds! From where the north-wind strows
  Blossoms that crown 'the King of Wisdom's' tomb,
  The trees here planted bring remembered bloom,
Dreaming in seed of Love's ancestral rose,
To meadows where a braver north-wind blows
  O'er greener grass, o'er hedge-rose, may, and broom,
  And all that make East England's field-perfume
Dearer than any fragrance Persia knows.

Hear us, ye winds, North, East, and West, and South!
This granite covers him whose golden mouth
  Made wiser ev'n the Word of Wisdom's King:
Blow softly over Omar's Western herald
  Till roses rich of Omar's dust shall spring
From richer dust of Suffolk's rare FitzGerald.

THEODORE WATTS-DUNTON (1832–1914)

The Old Vicarage, Grantchester

(*Café des Westens, Berlin, May 1912*)

Just now the lilac is in bloom,
All before my little room;
And in my flower-beds, I think,
Smile the carnation and the pink;
And down the borders, well I know,
The poppy and the pansy blow . . .
Oh! there the chestnuts, summer through,
Beside the river make for you
A tunnel of green gloom, and sleep
Deeply above; and green and deep
The stream mysterious glides beneath,
Green as a dream and deep as death.
—Oh, damn! I know it! and I know
How the May fields all golden show,
And when the day is young and sweet,
Gild gloriously the bare feet
That run to bathe . . .

Du lieber Gott!

Here am I, sweating, sick, and hot,
And there the shadowed waters fresh
Lean up to embrace the naked flesh.
Temperamentvoll German Jews
Drink beer around;—and *there* the dews
Are soft beneath a morn of gold.
Here tulips bloom as they are told;
Unkempt about those hedges blows
An English unofficial rose;
And there the unregulated sun
Slopes down to rest when day is done,
And wakes a vague unpunctual star,

A slippered Hesper; and there are
Meads towards Haslingfield and Coton
Where *das Betreten*'s not *verboten*.

εἴθε γενοίμην . . . would I were
In Grantchester, in Grantchester!—
Some, it may be, can get in touch
With Nature there, or Earth, or such.
And clever modern men have seen
A Faun a-peeping through the green.
And felt the Classics were not dead,
To glimpse a Naiad's reedy head,
Or hear the Goat-foot piping low: . . .
But these are things I do not know.
I only know that you may lie
Day-long and watch the Cambridge sky,
And, flower-lulled in sleepy grass,
Hear the cool lapse of hours pass,
Until the centuries blend and blur
In Grantchester, in Grantchester. . . .
Still in the dawnlit waters cool
His ghostly Lordship swims his pool,
And tries the strokes, essays the tricks,
Long learnt on Hellespont, or Styx.
Dan Chaucer hears his river still
Chatter beneath a phantom mill.
Tennyson notes, with studious eye,
How Cambridge waters hurry by . . .
And in that garden, black and white,
Creep whispers through the grass all night;
And spectral dance, before the dawn,
A hundred Vicars down the lawn;
Curates, long dust, will come and go
On lissom, clerical, printless toe;
And oft between the boughs is seen

The sly shade of a Rural Dean . . .
Till, at a shiver in the skies,
Vanishing with Satanic cries,
The prim ecclesiastic rout
Leaves but a startled sleeper-out,
Grey heavens, the first bird's drowsy calls,
The falling house that never falls.

God! I will pack, and take a train,
And get me to England once again!
For England's the one land, I know,
Where men with Splendid Hearts may go;
And Cambridgeshire, of all England,
The shire for Men who Understand;
And of *that* district I prefer
The lovely hamlet Grantchester.
For Cambridge people rarely smile,
Being urban, squat, and packed with guile;
And Royston men in the far South
Are black and fierce and strange of mouth;
At Over they fling oaths at one,
And worse than oaths at Trumpington,
And Ditton girls are mean and dirty,
And there's none in Harston under thirty,
And folks in Shelford and those parts
Have twisted lips and twisted hearts,
And Barton men make Cockney rhymes,
And Coton's full of nameless crimes,
And things are done you'd not believe
At Madingley, on Christmas Eve.
Strong men have run for miles and miles,
When one from Cherry Hinton smiles;
Strong men have blanched, and shot their wives,
Rather than send them to St. Ives;
Strong men have cried like babes, bydam,

To hear what happened at Babraham.
But Grantchester! ah, Grantchester!
There's peace and holy quiet there,
Great clouds along pacific skies,
And men and women with straight eyes,
Lithe children lovelier than a dream,
A bosky wood, a slumbrous stream,
And little kindly winds that creep
Round twilight corners, half asleep.
In Grantchester their skins are white;
They bathe by day, they bathe by night;
The women there do all they ought;
The men observe the Rules of Thought.
They love the Good; they worship Truth;
They laugh uproariously in youth;
(And when they get to feeling old,
They up and shoot themselves, I'm told) . . .
Ah God! to see the branches stir
Across the moon at Grantchester!
To smell the thrilling-sweet and rotten
Unforgettable, unforgotten
River-smell, and hear the breeze
Sobbing in the little trees.
Say, do the elm-clumps greatly stand
Still guardians of that holy land?
The chestnuts shade, in reverend dream,
The yet unacademic stream?
Is dawn a secret shy and cold
Anadyomene, silver-gold?
And sunset still a golden sea
From Haslingfield to Madingley?
And after, ere the night is born,
Do hares come out about the corn?
Oh, is the water sweet and cool,
Gentle and brown, above the pool?

And laughs the immortal river still
Under the mill, under the mill?
Say, is there Beauty yet to find?
And Certainty? and Quiet kind?
Deep meadows yet, for to forget
The lies, and truths, and pain? . . . oh! yet
Stands the Church clock at ten to three?
And is there honey still for tea?

RUPERT BROOKE (1887–1915)

Brooke once lived in the old Vicarage,
Grantchester, Cambridgeshire.